CONFIDENCE BOOSTER

How to Boost Confidence,
Set Boundaries and Practice
Self-Care in the
Changing Work World

HELENE LERNER

LIBRARY TALES PUBLISHING
www.LibraryTalesPublishing.com
www.Facebook.com/LibraryTalesPublishing

Copyright © 2022 by Helene Lerner
All Rights Reserved
Published in New York, New York.

For general information on our other products and services, please contact our Customer Care Department at 1-800-754-5016, or fax 917-463-0892. For technical support, please visit www.LibraryTalesPublishing.com

Library Tales Publishing also publishes its books in a variety of electronic formats. Every content that appears in print is available in electronic books.

978-1-956769-05-0
978-1-956769-06-7

PRINTED IN THE UNITED STATES OF AMERICA

CONTENTS

BIO

Helene Lerner is an Emmy award-winning executive producer, workplace consultant, prolific author of fourteen books, and founder of WomenWorking. com. As an inspiring influencer on social media, she has amassed a following of 19 million people. Helene began her career as a teacher, later working her way up through the management ranks of the New York Times. As CEO of Creative Expansions, Inc., a multimedia company, her mission is to empower women and girls.

This book is dedicated to all the courageous women who are on the front lines at work and at home, every day. You keep on keeping on, no matter what life throws at you. Your resiliency inspires me.

A special shout out to my wonderful Womenworking.com community for their words of wisdom and contribution of strong women quotes, some of which appear in this book.

The examples used in this book are compilations of real-life stories from women I've coached and interviewed.

WHY YOU NEED TO
READ THIS BOOK

I earned my stripes in the corporate workplace, working my way up the ranks of the *New York Times*. When I left the newspaper over two decades ago to start my own company, Creative Expansions, Inc., I had a mission to empower women in their work and their personal lives. My departure was even a surprise to me because the day I was supposed to return to work after maternity leave, I showed up at the Human Resources department in a trance-like state and instead of walking into my office, I resigned! This was unusual behavior for a calculated person, but my gut told me it was the right move at the time. My desire to make a significant impact in the health and well-being of women burned deep within my soul, and with a little help from my friends, I found the courage and confidence to create Womenworking.com. Years later, we have a social media following of over 19 million and growing.

Over the last two years, I have led virtual events for companies worldwide and have spoken to thousands of women. I'm seeing too many smart, compassionate women drained and on the verge of burnout. I call them heroes because they are on the front lines for their families, at work, and in their community. But when it comes to their own self-care, all too often, caring for others comes first.

COVID-19 has been hard on everyone, but especially women. Studies from *Catalyst* as well as McKinsey & Company and LeanIn.Org show that some women have considered downsizing their jobs or even leaving the workplace altogether.[1,2] Managing childcare and eldercare as well as full-time jobs throughout a catastrophic pandemic has been challenging, to say the least. But we don't want this phenomenon to feed into the bias about women advancing in the workplace.

Here lies the "rub"! All too often, managers may falsely believe that women cannot be C-Suite leaders because of their dual responsibilities, so when promotional decisions are made, women may not be considered. Companies are now facing labor shortages and there's a "war for talent." Women are an important part of the talent pool, so organizations should be responsible for providing flexible work arrangements for both women and men. They need to meet the demands of a rigorous lifestyle that involves job advancement, family responsibilities, and self-care. In May of 2021, *Catalyst* released a study suggesting that flexible work arrangements increase productivity and curb burnout.[3]

1. "The Detrimental Impact of Covid-19 on Gender and Racial Equality (Quick Take)." Catalyst, December 2020.

2. "Women in the Workplace 2020." September 2020, McKinsey & Company and LeanIn. Org, www.womenintheworkplace.com. Copyright (c) 2020 McKinsey & Company and LeanIn.Org. All rights reserved.

3. "Remote-Work Options Can Boost Productivity and Curb Burnout (Report)." Catalyst, May 2021.

McKinsey & Company and LeanIn.Org's "Women in the Workforce" report speaks to the intersectionality of women and the need for companies to acknowledge and reward them for their strong leadership. Corporations need to invest in all aspects of diversity, equity, and inclusion:

> Despite this added stress and exhaustion, women are rising to the moment as stronger leaders and taking on the extra work that comes with this: compared to men at the same level, women are doing more to support their teams and advance diversity, equity, and inclusion efforts. They are also more likely to be allies to women of color. Yet this critical work is going unrecognized and unrewarded by most companies, and that has concerning implications. Companies risk losing the very leaders they need right now, and it's hard to imagine organizations navigating the pandemic and building inclusive workplaces if this work isn't truly prioritized."[4]

With the ever-changing landscape of a hybrid workplace, new opportunities and challenges are popping up. The stress of re-entry into the workforce is escalating as different strains of the COVID-19 virus continue to emerge and create uncertainty. Workers are concerned about their kids and are anxious about their parent's health, many of whom live in different locations.

---

4. "Women in the Workplace 2021", September 2021, McKinsey & Company and LeanIn. Org, www.womeninthoworkplace.com. Copyright (c) 2020 McKinsey & Company and LeanIn.Org. All rights reserved.

Besides the issues of employee well-being and the safety of their families, career advancement needs to be addressed. Managers are now dealing with a combination of virtual and in-office employees, giving rise to new forms of potential workplace inequalities. For example, in staff meetings, people on Zoom may lose visibility to those who are physically in the room, so the question is - if you're working virtually, will you be able to attract the mentors and sponsors necessary for advancement?

Confidence Kick-Starter

If working virtually, indicate that you'd like to speak first in a hybrid meeting—then you don't take a back seat.

The world as we knew it has been turned upside down. And as a result, our confidence may be diminished. **How can we boost our confidence, set boundaries, and keep self-care a priority?** This is the sixty-four-thousand-dollar question! I have been working with and empowering women for years and have developed a five-step program to address this problem:

Step 1. Getting Clear on What You Want
Step 2. Speaking Up
Step 3. Knowing When to Let Go
Step 4. Creating Boundaries
Step 5. Keep Taking Smart Risks

Let's get started and explore the first step.

PART I
The Five-Step Program

Stepping out of your comfort zone
can be empowering. Dare to take
some "smart risks."

STEP 1: Getting Clear on What You Want

As working women, we are so used to taking care of everyone else—our families, our friends, our work responsibilities—that our own needs often get lost in the shuffle.

Does this sound familiar?

> *"Why do I have a splitting headache at 5pm? Oh, I forgot to take lunch!"*
>
> *"Sorry, can't speak right now! I'm with my daughter who is hysterical because a kid bullied her at school today!"*
>
> *"My boss insists I be at the 7:30 am meeting, no exercise this morning!"*

I like to use the analogy of an accordion. Just think of its movement: you pull it out, and then it comes back in. We are like that too: we give out so much of our own energy, but then we must come back in to recharge! Many of us fail to realize that when we give up our own self-care, in the end, our whole family and our work suffer, because we are more prone to getting sick. Self-care is not just a luxury, but a **necessity.**

Yes, crises do come up that must be attended to, but sometimes saying "No" to certain obligations, which are not really that important or critically urgent, is good for our own well-being (and sanity!). Saying NO and setting boundaries with people at home and at work is like saying YES to yourself. We will explore this further in Step 4.

"Self-care is not always a long vacation. It can be a small moment we give ourselves throughout the day, like a walk, a soothing bath, or a phone call with a friend."

— Helene Lerner

In the new hybrid work setting, we all have to do the best we can to manage change without any real guidelines. Whether we're the ones leading the company or just starting out, we've had to exercise intuitive muscles which we may not have known we had.

With all the changes that have come about, feeling overwhelmed is often a common occurrence. However, despite the confusion, there are still opportunities to vocalize our needs and to make our work environment more accommodating. This is the time to negotiate for yourself and let your voice be heard. But first, we must be very specific about what we need and prioritize our choices. Then, we can strategize the best way to go about getting what's needed now.

So, what exactly do YOU need right now to make your job easier and decrease your stress?

The experiences you've gone through during the pandemic will probably shape what you need. So, ask yourself: *What have I learned in these last two years? What has the pandemic taught me?*

Shelby, a high-level manager, explained:

At first, I was uncomfortable working alone in my apartment—I don't have kids and am single. But I spent time reflecting on my life and realized that my work schedule of 12-hour days was impacting my health. I was depleted. I began to do yoga and learned how to meditate—my team became accustomed to not calling me before 9 am. I let them know that I needed some "quiet" time. Frankly, I'll be working at the company's headquarters soon, and I feel anxious because I'm not sure if I'll be able to sustain my self-care routine."

I encouraged Shelby to stay with it because she will become more efficient, not less so, by taking care of herself.

During the pandemic, I realized the importance of making room for personal time. Although I love my work, I realized how fragile life is, and that *now* is the time to keep those appointments with friends so I can live a more balanced life. I also didn't realize how important my morning "swim" had been until our Health Club closed during quarantine. Even though I substituted walking for water aerobics, it wasn't the same.

What was your biggest lesson?

Shelby learned the importance of her daily self-care routine. Although she may feel shaky about maintaining it going back into a corporate setting, she was ready to negotiate. She met with her manager, and the company has agreed to meet her terms. She has negotiated working three days in-person with her team at company headquarters and two days from home.[5]

---

5. The examples I've used in this book are compilations of real-life stories from women I've coached and interviewed.

Not all companies may be as flexible as Shelby's, but there is still room to negotiate the things that are important to you.

Now it's your turn: Identify one item that you want; something important to you.

What is it?

Before you approach your manager, you must solidify a few things. I assume what you chose has a high level of importance. Now, consider this: is what you are asking for **non-negotiable** or is it **negotiable**?

If it is negotiable, what compromises are acceptable to you? Shelby's boss could have asked her to work one day remotely and four days starting at 9 am, in-person. For Shelby, this set-up would be flexible enough to accommodate her self-care needs, and she probably would have gone along with it. However, if her boss required her to start her day at 7:30 am three days a week to be part of an early morning global meeting, then it likely would not have been acceptable, as there would be no time for meditation and yoga—two activities that have become extremely important to her. If her boss had insisted, she might have had to start looking for a position elsewhere.

With the item you identified, is the request non-negotiable or are there areas you are willing to negotiate?

Write down the different scenarios that might arise. How do you think your boss might respond: definitely "no," a series of objections without a definite "no," or agreement. Of course, if it is an agreement, congratulate yourself for acting and getting what you need. If you project a series of objections, list what they might be. Here's a possible scenario.

If your "ask" is negotiable

Say you have an ailing father, and in the next few months, you will need to be flexible about working from home and in the office. Your father lives with you now, and *you will have to make yourself available for doctor appointments* (the "Ask").

Although sympathetic, your boss may object because...

• The team is coming back on certain days, and it is important for you to be there at those times.

• You are being considered for a promotion, and if you get it, it will necessitate your being at staff meetings with the higher-ups at least once a week, and your being on call for emergency meetings.

Now, counter each objection with a short sentence. Brevity is best!

Your response: *I can be with the team at least twice a week.*

Your response: *I will be at the meeting with the higher-ups and will only not be there if there is an emergency with my father.*

Setting up the meeting with your manager

Be strategic. When is it best to approach your supervisor —morning or afternoon? Ask to speak to your manager during the time that you think they will be most receptive. Make sure they know it's about a personal issue that will help you do your job better. Set the meeting for half an hour, not more.

Now that it's on your calendar…

Don't do it alone!

Identify a support buddy who can role-play your scheduled conversation with you prior to the meeting. Perhaps this person is a coworker that you trust or maybe a friend who is savvy in business. Once you've identified the person, make sure to stress that the relationship between the two of you is mutual, that you will be there for them when they need support. For the immediate future, set aside a half hour for this role-play. In Step Two, we will get into specifics of how to create a successful role-playing session.

Your support buddy is also a great person with whom to "book-end" your actions, meaning that you can touch base with them before you meet your boss, and then be able to let them know what happened after the meeting.

To combat any internal resistance that may come up…

There is a spiritual principle that when we move forward in our lives or try something new, the pull of the past is strong and can create resistance. It's important to prepare for this. Do this by remembering how important it is for you to speak up—it is not only serving you, but it is important for your family and the people at work.

Are you ready to step out of your comfort zone and get what you truly need to make your work-life more manageable and successful? Of course, the answer is YES! So read on and take Step Two.

Confidence Kick-Starter
Take on a new Mantra and repeat
it to yourself several times during
the day: "I am worthy of what I'm
asking for. I deserve the best, and
nothing less."

STEP 2: Speaking Up

This step is about speaking up and voicing your needs appropriately.

Why has it been difficult for some women to speak up?

Because women entered the workforce later than men, we've had to prove our capabilities, time and time again, having to be twice as good as our male counterparts. Yes, we have advanced through the years, but not quickly enough, as there are still too few women at the top leading organizations. Bias in the business world, as well as our own self-doubt about whether we can achieve the ambitious goals we set for ourselves, can keep us stuck. As a result, we may hold onto negative beliefs.

These beliefs are what I call "mad mind chatter," and they can stop us from speaking up and acting on our own behalf. I talk about this in my book, *Confidence Myth*.[6] As women, we may be telling ourselves lies that we internalized from the behavior of a teacher, a parent, an ex-boss, or even our current boss. For example, you may be telling yourself, *If I voice what's important, I'll be disappointed because my boss doesn't value what I say.* However, the reality is that you don't know *how* your supervisor will respond to your recommendation. If you focus on this negative belief, it most likely will lead to inaction, and you may stop yourself from getting what is necessary for your well-being. So you owe it to yourself to explore the negative beliefs that are getting in your

6. Lerner, Helene. *The Confidence Myth: Why Women Undervalue Their Skills and How to Get Over It.* Berrett-Koehler Publishers, Incorporated, a BK Business Book, 2015.

way, with the intention of letting them go.

Look inside

First, identify the "higher-up" with whom you will have to negotiate. It could be your boss, their supervisor, or someone else in a senior-level position. Next, ask yourself if you have any assumptions about the person that may stop you from letting them know what you need. For example, maybe the negative belief is: *My boss favors my coworker and doesn't pick up on my suggestions.* Take a moment to write down the belief that applies to your situation.

Is there a feeling attached to this belief? When we delve deeper, we usually find that there is. In the example I gave, the feeling attached is anger*: It infuriates me that he doesn't acknowledge my ideas—he's so dismissive.* What is the *feeling* attached to your negative belief?

Ghosts of the past

Ask yourself if the person you will be making your pitch to reminds you of anyone from your past—a parent, a family member, a teacher, an ex-boss, etc. If so, then it's likely that the feelings you associate with your current supervisor are reminiscent of them.

Recall an experience you had with this person from your past that was hurtful. Write it down.

> *What was the situation?*
> *Who was involved?*
> *What lies about yourself did you develop because of this incident?*

Sometimes it helps to share your insights with a trusted friend to ease the pain of remembrance. Also, therapy can be useful in working through these old wounds.

For example, Jane revealed to me a time when she was 11 years old:

> My father was angry when we were leaving for my elementary school graduation because I was late. He was screaming that I would never amount to anything! *I believed him.* Years later, after undergoing psychotherapy, I uncovered the fact that he was an alcoholic and I realized that he had projected his frustrations onto me. But this incident has left me scarred.

What about the historical person you've identified? Did you believe their messages about you? Do you now realize what they were saying about you were "lies," and they were projecting their frustrations onto you?

The next exercise can be transformative because it reaffirms that your needs matter and you are worthy of having them met.

Exercise: Create four columns on a piece of paper and label them with the following:

- Who is involved?
- What am I telling myself?
- Where does my belief stem from?
- What is the price I pay for thinking this way?

If we use the example given in the "Look inside" section, it would go something like this…

- Who is involved? *My boss and myself.*
- What am I telling myself? *My boss is dismissive and does not value what I say but instead favors my coworker.*
- Where does my belief stem from? *My father who put me down when I was a kid.*
- What is the price I pay for believing this? *I don't discuss what I need, and my needs don't get met.*

Using this chart, fill in your example and answer the questions. You are in the process of breaking down your "mad mind chatter" and exchanging lies for the truth.

So, what price did Jane pay for holding on to her falsehoods? She shared with me that by not speaking up, she was powerless to get what she really needed: "No one is a magician; they won't know what's best for me if I don't tell them."

As you uncover old "wounds" and start to let them go, you are likely to become more confident. But you may run up against other falsehoods that can chip away at your self-esteem. Let's explore these.

Unhealthy comparisons

There are times when we might compare ourselves to people who seem more confident or more successful than us. We may tell ourselves that we should be able to achieve what they have! But we just waste our time and energy with these comparisons. The people that seem so sure of themselves usually aren't. All we accomplish by comparing ourselves to others is to deplete our energy and decrease our self-esteem.

Be truthful and ask yourself: *Do I compare myself to other people and keep falling short?* Unfortunately, by reinforcing this comparative behavior, we feel less confident, and as a result, may pull back and not ask for what we need.

The more we disengage from our "harsh" inner critic that tells us that nothing we do is good enough, the more we are empowered to get what we need in our career and our personal lives.

Redefining confidence

In *The Confidence Myth,* I suggest that confidence is not the "absence of fear, but our ability to move through fear." Many women leaders I've interviewed through the years took calculated risks because it was the right course of action, but that doesn't mean they didn't have trepidation. My definition of confidence is:

Moving forward when you think you can make a difference, change a conversation for the better, offer up an idea—you're not sure if it's going to fly, but you do it because you believe it's important—even with shaky knees!

It's time to speak up

Courage, conviction, and the desire to make a difference will propel you forward. By knowing that "shaky knees" is par for the course, you'll face your fear and do it anyway! Whether it's shaky knees or a shaky voice—it doesn't really matter. Those around you are probably so busy worrying about themselves that they won't even notice.

So, feel your fear, and step up anyway to negotiate what you need. Use your support buddy for feedback.

Get clear on the communication style of your boss

It is a good practice to know the different communication styles of the people you deal with at work. There are many elaborate ways to analyze these styles, but I use a basic one. Some managers use a few words, numbers, or charts to make their points. Interactions with these types of people are usually short and specific. Then, there are managers who are storytellers. Communicating with them may be a bit longer because they use descriptive examples.

Identify the communication style of your manager. Also, observe the words or phrases your supervisor uses frequently and try to incorporate them into your conversations.

Role-play *before* your meeting

You have identified a support buddy in Step One, and you've set time for a role-playing session before you meet with your boss.

Come prepared to the meeting with your buddy by having practiced your pitch to your boss in the mirror a few times. Ask yourself as you are practicing: *am I sincere and clear about what I am asking for?*

Tips for the role-playing session with your support buddy

In your pitch, use short sentences and don't over-explain. After you finish a sentence, take a breath. Even if it feels awkward, don't say anything. Leave room for your boss (or support buddy) to make a comment.

Regarding your "ask," know which points are non-negotiable and which ones are flexible. Throughout the role-playing session with your buddy, take in their feedback. Don't be defensive. Feel free to ask them questions if you are unsure of something they say. You may think you are being clear, but maybe that's not how you're coming across. Also, ask them if you are leaving enough space for your boss to respond.

In the actual session with your boss, if all goes well, you will be able to get your points across and negotiate what's needed, or you will have a follow-up meeting to counter their objections.

But if you have a particularly difficult boss, how do you effectively communicate with them?

We've all met them, and if you have one, they can make your life miserable.

Appeal to their expertise—perhaps a project or campaign they are working on that might tie into your request. For example, if senior leadership is concerned about retaining employees, you might want to mention that you decided to speak up because the work you are doing for the company and your career with them is extremely important to you.

Show them right away how your "ask" can increase retention. Propose a schedule to meet with them regularly to assess how things are going. Make sure they know you are open to any changes that will need to be made along the way. For instance, if the "ask" is to have "coffee meet-ups" on Friday with leaders from the company, let your boss know that setting this up for the team gives people the opportunity to be introduced to potential sponsors or mentors. Not only will leaders share what works and what doesn't about advancement, but this tactic is in line with retaining talent, which is one of the company's objectives.

Confidence Kick-Starter
Give yourself a pat on the back for engaging in a difficult conversation, no matter what the outcome is.

STEP 3: Knowing When to Let Go

Hopefully, when you meet with your boss, the response to your "ask" will be "yes." However, the result may not always be that positive.

Nobody likes being turned down, especially when it takes a lot to muster up the courage to raise an issue with your supervisor. Hearing "no" uttered from your boss's mouth stings! But did you really have a choice not to say anything?

The price you pay by remaining silent is too great. Not speaking up on important issues can make you resentful of those who do, and it can create a "victim" mentality which will sap your productive energy and keep you from getting what you need. When we don't own our feelings or let others know our truth, our relationships suffer. Withholding information about our needs can destroy our ability to have close connections with people.

As if we don't have enough stress in our lives! We may think that stress is a normal part of everyday life, but it isn't. We are stressed because we are "stressable."[7] It's not the situations in our lives that cause us stress, but our reactions to them. So, if you are reacting out of "fear" and wondering what the consequence of your speaking up would be, you will probably be less prone to acting. What's the worst-case scenario? You are turned down! You'll deal with it.

A high-level manager once shared with me how angry she was after her boss rejected an important request:

---

7. Lerner, Helene, and Roberta Elins. *Stress Breakers*. Hazelden, 1995.

"I was on the pity-pot that night, letting myself feel my feelings, bitching to my best friend, but by the next day, I moved on. There was no point in holding on to my rage."

She gave herself a night to process her feelings. Then, after a certain point, she knew it was best to let it go.

When we get a "no," we may deny our feelings to protect ourselves. But if we are not aware, our negative thoughts can pile up and lead to other problems. We may find ourselves enraged over something totally unrelated that seems trivial, or suddenly experience body pains that weren't there a few weeks ago.

If your boss has turned you down, process your disappointment when you have some quiet time. Ask yourself: *What are you feeling?* Is it anger? Fear? Identify any tension in your body. Are your shoulders tight? Do you have neck pain? *What can you do right now to support yourself?* Maybe it's calling a friend and openly talking about how you feel. Whatever you need to do to release your negative thoughts, do it. And distance from the incident will help.

Hearing "no" is a small price to pay for having the courage to let people know the real you.

I've noticed that successful people keep asking for what they need, whether they get it or not. They seem to have developed a thick skin for when they are turned down.

It helps to understand the context of why your request was turned down, and to inquire further about what the "no" means—*Not now? Never?* Try to get as much clarity as you can from your boss, so you will know how to proceed in the future. Unfortunately, if your boss is withholding, you may never find out.

Possible reasons for a "no"

• Purely arbitrary

• Competing priorities

• Money issues

• You are needed for other things

"No" signals that the situation is out of your control. For example, your boss may be doing something else that's competing with what you asked. Or maybe your timing is off—it's a good idea, but not right now. They may also just flatly say "no." The following are different types of "noes" that you may hear.

"Not now"

"No" may mean, "not right now." It's not the right timing, and your "ask" can be addressed again in the future. When you are talking with your supervisor, you can get clarification by asking, "Can we revisit this in three months?" Wait for a response.

"Never"

In other cases, "no" may mean that your "ask" is not going to happen on your manager's watch. If the "ask" remains important to you, there is a factor to consider: Will there be a change of supervisors soon? Just because this person said "no," it does not mean the next supervisor will. If you have history with the company and the job is fulfilling your other needs, it's probably worth it to stay and see if things change. You can stick it out for now, and reevaluate your goals and overall job satisfaction again later. It's never too late to make the best decision for you.

To review: When you get a "no," don't run from the feelings through busyness or apathy. Give yourself a set amount of time to process your feelings. Then ask yourself: *Will holding on get me anywhere?* The answer is clearly "no," so acknowledge that you did speak up, and say to yourself, "Next!"

When you let go, you are showing your supervisor that you're a team player, that you're thinking of what's best overall—even if you don't agree with it. So be strategic and put yourself in a good light with the people in charge.

Confidence Kick-Starter
They say that the more "noes" you receive, the closer you are to the "yes." So keep putting yourself out there.

STEP 4: Creating Boundaries

Whether you received the answer you wanted in Step Two or not, being clear about what you need is necessary to create a life according to your own design. For many, the pandemic has brought to the surface the need to find a harmony between work and personal life, and creating realistic boundaries is key to achieving this.

In my generation, women were raised to be "nice," to want to please at all costs. Graciousness is a wonderful quality, but if we take it to the extreme, we may cross over the line and find ourselves "people-pleasing," as I talk about in my book, *Time for Me: A Burst of Energy for Busy Women,* trying to seduce someone to like us, at the price of losing ourselves in the process. [8]

The truth

We can't be all things to all people, and although we may want approval, not everyone will like us, no matter what we do. If we become more truthful about our desires and needs, we may lose some people. For example, if someone is used to your saying "yes," when you start saying "no," they may get agitated and argumentative. Nevertheless, when we set boundaries, our giving is more honest, and we are taking care of ourselves.

---

8. Lerner, Helene. *Time for Me: A Burst of Energy for Busy Women.* Sourcebooks, Inc., 2005.

I want you to think about these questions:

- Do you set clear boundaries with people?
- Are your conversations really honest?
- Do you say "yes" when you want to say "yes" and say "no" when you want to say "no"?

It is uncomfortable to set limits if you run the risk of losing someone when you are truthful. But as we are more honest, our "yeses" become more meaningful. Saying "no" is saying "yes" to yourself.

Alice shared with me that she was the "go-to" person for her extended family for favors or taking charge of activities. When they needed someone, she was the one! Whether it was planning family celebrations or hosting holiday dinners, she ended up taking it on. And she didn't receive much help; they just assumed she would do what was needed. Recently, she was put in charge of a family Zoom event, and they assumed she'd pull it off in a month. Alice works a full-time job, her daughter was newly-engaged, and she wanted to go on a mini-vacation with her husband. She was exhausted and confided in me, "Why am I doing this? I asked for help, and no one came forward." She thought about her motives for accepting the assignment and then admitted, "I like the 'strokes' and compliments I get by being in charge, but it's not worth the stress I am putting myself under." She decided not to do another event. "They'll get someone else—they'll have to." And to finish off her current commitment, she asked persistently for help, and got it!

Get comfortable with the uncomfortable

New behavior is uncomfortable, but like exercising your physical muscles, it becomes easier the more you do it. I have heard several leaders advise that, when you are too comfortable, you do not challenge yourself or grow. What I have learned to do in saying "no," is to be honest and sympathetic to the person's needs.

1. Let them know you would like to help, but you have too much on your plate right now.

2. Give them an alternative: Mention someone else who may be able to help.

3. You may want to offer to help them with something else in the future. Ask them to call on you in two weeks if they need a favor.

Confidence Kick-Starter
When you set boundaries with people, you begin to know who your real friends are.

STEP 5: Keep Taking Smart Risks

In the previous steps, we've learned to identify, prioritize, and speak up to get our needs met. These days, continuous action is required because everything is changing so rapidly.

Claim your strength

As you start to regularly negotiate your needs, you will find that you have more energy to do the things that are important to you. Old habits may come back—like feeling guilty for prioritizing your needs over other's. Too many women I coach tell me about the guilt they feel when they do good things for themselves. We are wired to take care of other people. **Give up the guilt!** It only serves to keep you stuck. You will never be able to please everyone, so don't second-guess your choices. Instead, get back on track, face your fears and keep moving forward.

How do you determine if speaking up on an issue is a risk worth taking?

I will offer you a way to do just that based on how I've analyzed taking risks in my life. Perhaps you already use this method, so this may serve as a good review. I expand on this in my book, *Smart Women Take Risks.*[9]

1. Look at the advantages and disadvantages of speaking up on the issue. Write them down in list form, the pluses and the minuses.

---

9. Lerner, Helene. *Smart Women Take Risks: Six Steps for Conquering Your Fears and Making the Leap to Success.* McGraw-Hill, 2006.

2. Add up the columns. Which has the highest number of entries?

3. Using a scale of 1 to 5, with 1 being least important to you, and 5 being most, rank each entry.

4. Add up the numbers.

5. Now, which column has the most points?

Based on your list, you should have an idea of whether to take that risk–whether it is voicing an issue of concern or taking on a new project.

Remember, no one has all the answers—especially people in charge. In these days of uncertainty, taking smart risks is about using our best judgment and letting our intuition guide us to take grounded actions. That small voice within me has helped me out many times. As I wrote in *The Confidence Myth:*

> When you follow your inner compass, you feel more confident taking the smart risks necessary to advance [your career and your life]. Listen to your inner voice and use it to help you make better decisions that will benefit you, the people you serve, and your company.

Take Andrea as an example. She used the 20 months away from her corporate location to delve deeply and reevaluate what she did not have in her life. She and her husband had been trying to have a child, but it didn't happen. They decided to adopt instead, and now they've expanded to a family of three. Although her mother is helping raise her child, she needs to establish firm boundaries at her corporate workplace, where she works in-person three days a week until 6pm. To deal with this issue, she arranged to have a conversation with her boss. She was nervous about the meeting because the "old Andrea" stayed around till 7pm, but no more! This move was a risk worth taking because she realized her needs were non-negotiable. Ultimately, her boss was supportive.

How do you determine whether the "ask" is important enough to bring up in your personal life?

The same method can be used in deciding whether to move forward on a risky action in your personal life. In Andrea's case, her life was turned upside down in more ways than one during her time away from the office. Aside from COVID-19, many changes took place when she and her husband decided to expand their family. It was uncomfortable asking her husband to participate more in responsibilities at home, as she wasn't sure what his reaction would be. He also worked full-time, yet still expected her to do the brunt of the chores at home. With the support of a friend, she weighed the consequences and decided to raise the issue and talk with him. He was reluctant but understood, so now she negotiates the little things with him daily. She told me that speaking up became easier over time. Andrea and her husband don't always agree, but she isn't backing down.

Keep creating your life powerfully

It is up to us to take the actions to get what we want. It's so easy to fall back and think that circumstances have been responsible for our good luck or misfortune, but this type of thinking is deceptive. We have choices about how we want to live our lives, and every day we make decisions that create our reality.

Don't do it alone. Reach out for help—enlist those support buddies who will "coach you to win." Be a mirror for other women and support them as they move through their challenges.

To speaking up!

To getting our needs met!

To taking smart risks!

To being healthy!

To having an impact!

To all strong women: the world needs every bit of your resourcefulness. Step up!

Confidence Kick-Starter
The time to take action is now!
Don't let anyone or anything
dissuade you.

PART II
Change Your Perspective

Now that you have taken my five-step program to boost confidence in this rapidly changing hybrid workplace, the following pages offer additional tools to turn "mad mind chatter" around. You'll find positive ways of looking at challenging situations, empowering quotes, and actions to keep you moving forward in your life.

Flip It Around

Even the best leaders get sidetracked with fear and worry. We must be conscious of our negative mind-talk—the lies that we may believe are true—and turn them around.

Here are some of them…

Lie: *I have lost momentum at work being home for so long. Am I going to be able to advance in my career?*

Flip it: *I did what was needed at home, and now I can focus on my next career steps.*

Lie: *I am overwhelmed and can't take action. New virus strains are emerging, and kids are back in school. I worry for their safety.*

Flip it: *Most people are feeling the same way, even if our circumstances are different. I need to focus on what's in front of me and take the next right action.*

Lie: *I am drained emotionally and physically. We usually go on a few vacations during the year, but we haven't this year. I feel like I can't replenish.*

Flip it: *I can do one thing a day towards self-care and make that non-negotiable. It doesn't have to take much time or cost much money.*

Lie: *My parents live in another state—I should visit them regularly but can't because of my job responsibilities. I feel guilty and irresponsible.*

Flip it: *Guilt serves no purpose and will sap my energy. I can have regular Zoom sessions with my parents. If I am needed in an emergency, I will be there.*

Think Positive

Old way: *I have been asked to take the lead but I have never been in charge of so many people. I am not sure I can do it.*

New scenario: *Of course I can do it. I will give it a shot. If I make a mistake, I have my network for support and will try again.*

Old way: *I am exhausted. My son had COVID-19, but now he is okay. Still, I am worried. My job is demanding, as well. There is too much on my plate and I'm overwhelmed.*

New scenario: *I can organize my time better and look at what absolutely must get done in a day and leave the rest. My team has offered to help, so I will give them what I can't do.*

Old way: *Dad is alone in the house during the day, and I'm at work while my kids are in high school. I'm worried about him. Mom died a few months back, and he is depressed. I think about him way too much at work.*

New scenario: *I can set check-in times with him to see how he is doing, and make sure that I speak with him at least twice a day. When I'm not checking in, I will focus on the work at hand.*

Old way: *I know what's needed but I haven't offered my ideas because I don't believe my boss will take me seriously. He's critical, and it seems like nothing I do is right!*

New scenario: *Whatever is going on with my boss is none of my business. If I know a solution to a problem, I will let him know, regardless of what his reaction might be.*

Old way: *My daughter is having problems adjusting to school, and I may have to be on call a few days a week. Although my boss says he's flexible, he usually gives me a hard time. I'm nervous about approaching him.*

New scenario: *Family first. My child is having a hard time, so I will make sure that I approach my boss tomorrow. This is non-negotiable.*

Old way: *I'm in the office twice a week, and some of my coworkers are there, full-time.*

They are getting more face time with our boss. I don't want to lose momentum on my career advancement, but I'm not sure how to stand out.

New scenario: *A coach suggested that when we have meetings with our hybrid team, I make sure to comment at the beginning and voice an opinion, so that way I am adding something meaningful to the dialogue. I will give it a try.*

WISDOM FOR THE STRONG AT HEART

50 Reflections for Resilient Women

Leadership

**Today, I choose to think bigger
about what I can achieve.
I choose to live
as a leader and create impact.**

Leadership

"A strong woman knows that fear is part of the journey. But her commitment to making a difference is greater. Her motto: being of service trumps fear!"
~ Helene Lerner

Ask yourself:

Why not me?
Who knows better?

Act

Speak up now!

Strength

**I realize that to be strong
is to have the courage to
walk through the storms
life brings.**

Strength

"A strong woman knows she can handle whatever storm crosses her path, with a little help from her friends." - Helene Lerner

Ask yourself:

What gives me courage?
What was the last storm I walked through?

Act

Keep going and take the next right action!

Resiliency

**Cheers to strong women
around the world.
Let's toast to our resilience,
compassion, and greatness!**

Resiliency

"A strong woman turns down the volume of negative self-talk and doesn't pay attention to toxic people. She has important work to do, and will not be stopped from doing it." ~ Helene Lerner

Ask yourself:

How do I handle conflict?
Am I selective about negative feedback?
(I take what fits and leave the rest).

Act

Do one thing today that moves you a step closer to achieving your aspirations.

Breaking News

You were born to lead.
Anything you don't know now,
you will learn.
Don't doubt yourself.

Breaking News

"You are a leader who can have a great impact.
Acknowledge your power." ~ Helene Lerner

Ask yourself:

Have I brushed alongside someone with greatness?
What common qualities do I share
with them?

Act

Visualize yourself achieving something they have.
Know that it is possible for you to have it too.

Set Boundaries

Strong women set boundaries. They do not tolerate disrespect and they choose to be around supportive people.

Set Boundaries

"A strong woman realizes that she can't be all things to all people, and that saying "No" opens up an opportunity for someone else to fill the spot."
~ Helene Lerner

Ask yourself:

When have I tolerated less than I deserve?
What made me stop doing that?

Act

Use the word "no" when you need to.

Choice

Life will never be easy.
It is up to you to
choose how you show up for it.
Choose health.
Choose wealth.
Choose peace of mind.

Choice

"Being a strong woman means loving yourself when society says you're too big or too skinny or too dark or too tall or too short or too much or too little. It means defining your own strength."~ Ocha UchOgidi

Ask yourself:

When have I gotten through a tough time?
What helped me do that?

Act

Accept what cannot be changed
and change what you can.

Happiness

Happiness is about things money can't buy. It's about love, compassion, empathy, and the courage to face every day with a desire to have an impact. To make the lives of people around us a little bit better.

Happiness

"A strong woman gets pleasure from the little things in life, which she realizes are actually big things."
~ Helene Lerner

Ask yourself:

What was the happiest time of my life?
What steps can I take to reclaim my joy, every day?

Act

Whether it's big or small, do one
thing to brighten your day.

A Good Life

Wisdom, patience, faith, and laughter are the ingredients to a good life. Let your joy be contagious to those you encounter.

A Good Life

"You deserve the best, and nothing less. Go about your day knowing this to be true."~ Helene Lerner

Ask yourself:

*Have I lived today being the best I can be?
If not, why not?*

Act

Treat yourself well, not only for you, but because others look to you as a role model.

Show Up

No matter how you feel,
good or bad,
show up each day.
You never know the people
you will inspire.

Show Up

"Even on the 'hanging on' days, what gets me out of bed is the ability to be of service to others."
~ Helene Lerner

Ask yourself:

What gives me the strength to show up, even when I don't want to? How do I feel when I do?

Act

Fake it until you make it!
When you don't feel like being visible,
act as if you do, and take the next right action!

Life Lesson

**Never take anything for granted.
You will be terribly disappointed
if you do.**

Life Lesson

"Practicing gratitude can shift one's attitude from victim to victor." ~ Helene Lerner

Ask yourself:

Do I appreciate all I have?
If not, why not?

Act

Make a gratitude list of 3 things you are grateful for right now.

Peace

At the end of the day,
be at peace knowing that
you have done your best.

Peace

"You are enough, just the way you are."
~ Helene Lerner

Ask yourself:

Am I setting impossible standards for myself?
Have I tried my best today?

Act

Give yourself the credit you deserve.

Treasure

My greatest treasure is the people I love. Our love runs deep.

Treasure

"A strong woman loves the person in the mirror as much as she loves others." ~ Vicki Clark

Ask yourself:

Who have I taken for granted recently?
What would I like to tell them?

Act

Let someone know how much you appreciate them. Tell them exactly why.

Priorities

Don't waste your time
explaining yourself
to people who don't understand.

Priorities

*"You are your priority. If you don't take
care of yourself, no one else will." ~ Helene Lerner*

Ask yourself:

*Are there people in my life who don't take me
seriously? If so, who do they remind me of?*

Act

Change the channel.
Create relationships with people
who you want to be around.
The new story is so much better than the old one.

Equality

All beings on this planet deserve
respect and equal treatment:
the custodian, the CEO, the people
you have yet to meet.

Equality

"We may come from different backgrounds and do different jobs, but we all deserve respect and acknowledgment." ~ Helene Lerner

Ask yourself:

Do I take time out to acknowledge the people who serve me? Is 'thank you' part of my everyday vocabulary?

Act

Don't just tell someone you appreciate them. Show them by reciprocating in a small way.

Love

Share your love.
Don't hold back.
One person's kindness
can make a big difference.

Love

"A strong woman realizes that kindness is non-negotiable. She knows that love has the power to heal." ~ Helene Lerner

Ask yourself:

Do I realize that kindness is one of my greatest strengths? Am I quick to acknowledge someone who has been kind to me?

Act

Offer a kind word to someone in need.

Empathy

**Toxic people are hurting.
They probably will not tell you
what they are going through—
show compassion anyway.**

Empathy

"Our intuition can help us become more empathetic.
It allows us to see deeper than outward appearances."
~ Helene Lerner

Ask yourself:

Am I aware that rude people
are unhappy with themselves?
Do I tend to take things personally?

Act

Next time someone is rude, detach.
It has nothing to do with you.

Slow Down

**Exhaustion is both
a bodily state, as well as
a state of mind.
By slowing down, we nourish the
body and feed the soul.**

Slow down

"What we are chasing on the outside is never as important as our inner peace." ~ Helene Lerner

Ask yourself:

What keeps me on the treadmill?
If I slow down, what am I afraid will happen?

Act

Catch yourself when you are rushing around. The only fire that needs to be put out is in you.

Community

Best therapy in the world!
Talking with our biological
or unbiological sisters.

Community

"A woman's strength comes from who she surrounds herself with. Her tribe, her support system, collectively holds her up and makes her strong. We build our futures by helping others." ~ Irene Conlin

Ask yourself:

Who is my support system?
Are the women in my circle receiving my insights and support as well?

Act

Take a moment to reach out for support
when you need it today.

Know Your Worth

**Life's too short to spend time
with people who don't value you.
Instead, surround yourself
with people who do.**

Know Your Worth

"She is defined, not by others, but by her own principles, values, and self-worth. She may sacrifice some of what she has but gives up nothing by doing so." ~ Stacey Hill

Ask yourself:

*Do I give myself the credit I deserve?
Do I acknowledge the impact I have on others?*

Act

Acknowledge yourself by owning how much you've grown and how far you've come.

Perspective

There are so many people
who are worse off than you.
See how you can help and practice
gratitude throughout the day.

Perspective

"When my problems seem too great, I reach out and help someone else. I feel better when I do."
~ Helene Lerner

Ask yourself:

Do I realize I'm just a small cog in a big universal wheel? Do I look at the bigger picture to see what's needed?

Act

Use your time and talent to help someone in need.

Healing

Honor your grief.
Things change.
People come in and out of your life.
Sometimes we lose the people that
matter most.
Treat yourself with loving kindness.

Healing

"Crying can be a gift when it helps us heal."
~ Helene Lerner

Ask yourself:

Is it difficult for me to stay with uncomfortable feelings? Am I feeling sad and alone these days?

Act

Treat yourself as if you were your own young child: with compassion, love, and understanding.

Karma

What goes around,
comes around, they say.
When someone does you wrong,
know that karma has your back.

Karma

"Don't waste your energy with toxic people.
They will get what they deserve."
~ Helene Lerner

Ask yourself:

Do I give people too many chances when they act
poorly? Am I angry deep inside?

Act

Get clear on how you feel. Stick up for yourself.
Say what needs to be said.

Silence is Power

Silence sometimes means that I know better than to trust you. Sometimes, it is the best way of taking care of myself.

Silence is Power

*"I give people a lot of chances, but after a certain
point, it's not worth it. It's their loss."*
~ Helene Lerner

Ask yourself:

Instead of getting mad, do I get silent?
Do I use silence to manipulate people?

Act

Feel your feelings and if silence is appropriate,
keep your mouth shut.

Focus

**Worry drains and saps our energy.
Nip it in the bud, and go after
something important to you!**

Focus

"Catch your negative thinking and turn it around.
You have important work to do."
~ Helene Lerner

Ask yourself:

Do I overthink things?
Am I often exhausted by my own negative thoughts?

Act

Be aware of negative mind-talk.
Focus on something positive instead.

Recharge

**Even strong women get tired.
You have the right to rest.
Do something today that will
recharge your body and soul.**

Recharge

"Resting your mind and body is not a luxury, it's a must for busy women." ~ Helene Lerner

Ask yourself:

Do I take care of other people, at the expense of myself? Am I a giver, but have a hard time receiving?

Act

Pencil in ten minutes today and every day to sit quietly and do nothing.

Saying "No"

"No" is a two-letter word that
can transform your life.
Use it today so that your "yeses"
carry more value.

Saying "No"

*"Turning someone down takes courage,
and you may lose people when you do.
But what you gain is more important: yourself!"*
~ Helene Lerner

Ask yourself:

*Do I people-please and say "yes" when I really mean
"no"? Do I resent people for wanting
too much from me?*

Act

Change feels uncomfortable, but it signals growth.
Say "no" when it is appropriate, even if the other
person gets upset.

Falsehoods

The older I get, the more I realize
that my heart never lies, but
my head does.

Falsehoods

*"My mind plays tricks on me, it tells me a lot of lies.
I've learned not to listen to it."*
~ Helene Lerner

Ask yourself:

*Do I find myself fearful
much of the time?
Am I in touch with my intuition?*

Act

Today, take an action that comes from a deeper
place. Don't listen to your fear.

Breathe

When you feel like your head is spinning, stop what you are doing. Pause and take a deep breath, then proceed.

Breathe

"So many of us forget to breathe deeply when we're stressed. Instead, we get caught up in the current crisis which entangles us more." ~ Helene Lerner

Ask yourself:

Do I react to a challenging situation from an emotional place? Am I taking time to pause and think of what the next right action would be?

Act

When overwhelmed, take a time-out. Take a walk or call a friend. Getting away, even if only briefly, will help center you.

Begin Anew

Be aware of when you're retelling
an "old story" about yourself.
Isn't it boring?
Try on a new one for size!

Begin Anew

*"Imagine that you are meeting the people in your life
for the first time. Reintroduce yourself."*
~ Helene Lerner

Ask yourself:

*Do I call on old ways of being because they feel
comfortable? Are there people in my life that expect
me to act one way, and would be disturbed if I acted
differently?*

Act

When you catch yourself telling the same old
story, stop and dare to take on a new one!

Be Alert

There are givers and there are takers.
Watch for the takers that masquerade
as givers. Don't be fooled.

Be Alert

"You deserve nourishing relationships;
to receive as well as to give."
~ Helene Lerner

Ask yourself:

Am I the one that does the most giving in a
relationship? Am I resentful when I realize that the
other person is all "get" and no "give"?

Act

Express your feelings with "I" statements like
"I feel that I'm always doing things for you, but
when I ask you for something, you change the
subject. That's not okay with me."

Take Notice

The pandemic has taught
me that the little things
in life make me happy.

Take Notice

"What I've come to realize is that seeing a child's smile and listening to my favorite music after a rough day means so much, if I view it that way."
~ Helene Lerner

Ask yourself:

Do I feel unfulfilled lately?
Do I gloss over the little moments that really make life special?

Act

Be sure to take time out to do one thing today that makes you happy.

Reach Out

Sharing with a trusted friend when you feel vulnerable is a sign of strength, not weakness.

Reach Out

"A strong woman knows that her power lies in her ability to reach out for help." - Helene Lerner

Ask yourself:

Do I let people see all sides of me, or do I keep secrets? When I've shown a friend or colleague a different side of myself, what was their reaction?

Act

Let your guard down. Have a deeper conversation with one of your colleagues.

Don't Take it Personally

Don't get distracted by people who are stressed out. They may be having a harder time than you.

Don't Take it Personally

*"People who are hurting may want others to feel
the same way—misery loves company.
Don't get caught up in their drama." ~ Helene Lerner*

Ask yourself:

*Do I gossip and focus on the drama of negative
people? What work should I be doing that would be
more productive?*

Act

Don't participate in gossip or drama
—they are time wasters.

Make it Simple

Whether at work or at home, breaking things down into simple tasks is the way to get things done.

Make It Simple

*"Life gets easier when you don't complicate it.
If you believe there is a solution to a challenge, the
way will become clear." ~ Helene Lerner*

Ask yourself:

*Do I often make things more complicated than they
are? Am I willing to keep it simple?*

Act

Next time you are asked to do something complex,
break it down into small tasks and do one task
at a time.

Self-Acceptance

Accept all of your feelings without judgment:
your anger,
your fear,
your sadness,
your joy.

Self-Acceptance

"A strong woman has learned not to judge her feelings, actions, and reactions. She knows that at any moment in time, she is doing her best."
~ Helene Lerner

Ask yourself:

Am I overly critical of myself?
Do I accept some things about myself, but not others?

Act

List three qualities that you admire about yourself.

Embrace Yourself

See yourself as a young child,
a teenager, an adult.
Have compassion for each stage
of your life.

Embrace Yourself

"Sometimes we judge ourselves harshly and are our own worst critics. We need to praise ourselves more."
~ Helene Lerner

Ask yourself:

Am I thinking too much about what I "should" be doing? Is it hard to forgive myself for making a mistake?

Act

Look in the mirror and tell yourself,
"I did my best, and that is good enough!".

Step Up

Your talents and gifts can make
a difference in the lives of others.
Don't wait to share them.
When the need presents itself,
step up.

Step Up

"The real crime is when we do not use our talents and gifts—that's when depression can set in."
~ Helene Lerner

Ask yourself:

What is one of my talents I haven't used as much as I would like to? Do I hold back from sharing my special qualities with people? If so, why?

Act

When you have an impulse to give creatively, do it.

Appreciation

**Praise people like it's going out of
style. Everyone needs a boost these
days. Your words are powerful.
Use them to uplift.**

Appreciation

"Take note of the people who are there for you, from the grocery clerk, to the mailman, to the neighbor who says hello - the list goes on. These people make your day a little brighter." ~ Helene Lerner

Ask yourself:

Do I value the small ways people help me out?
Am I quick to praise people?

Act

Jot down three times you praised someone today.

Tolerance

Give people the benefit of the doubt. They are probably walking through their own storms.

Tolerance

"If someone lashes out at you, it's probably because they feel horrible about themselves." ~ Helene Lerner

Ask yourself:

Do I have a quick temper?
Can I give a person in a bad mood some slack?

Act

Realize the pandemic has taken a toll on all of us.
Offer a "random act of kindness" to
someone in need.

Reverse it

The critical mind is always chattering. Why not lower its volume and raise the volume on your positive thoughts.

Reverse It

"The real problem is that we know we are capable of so much more, but we let self-doubt get the upper hand." ~ Helene Lerner

Ask yourself:

Am I afraid to take a risk that I know I should be taking? Do I know I can feel the fear and move forward anyway?

Act

Take a calculated risk. Start by taking a small step towards reaching a stretch goal.

Now is the Time

**Things may never come together
exactly as you would like.
So why wait?
Ask yourself:
"Why not now?"**

Now is the Time

"What helps me step up when I'm afraid is focusing on the opportunity and how it will impact others in a positive way." ~ Helene Lerner

Ask yourself:

Do I feel stuck lately?
Do I second-guess myself?

Act

No one has it all together. Take the plunge. If an opportunity comes along, realize you can learn what you need on the job or delegate certain tasks to others.

Be Bold

When you are unsure of whether to take action or not, stop what you are doing. Take a deep breath and tune into your intuition, then act accordingly.

Be Bold

"Your intuition doesn't lie. Don't doubt it, no matter what evidence is to the contrary. Speak up."
~ Helene Lerner

Ask yourself:

Do I not offer my opinion because I think it won't be taken seriously? Are am I aware of how powerful I am?

Act

No matter how you feel, let your voice be heard.

Pay
Attention

Slow and steady wins the race,
but not always!
Sometimes fast and furious finishes
first. Let your intuition guide you.
You'll know exactly what to do and
when to do it.

Pay Attention

"Use what you know to read between the lines of what a person is saying. Tap into a deeper meaning."
~ Helene Lerner

Ask yourself:

Do I make decisions based upon my intuition?
When was the last time I "should" have listened to my gut, and regretted that I didn't?

Act

When in doubt, connect with the small voice within you. The answer will come.

Keep Moving Forward

We all have our fair share of
disappointments, like projects we
counted on that didn't pan out. How
do we turn these frustrations around?
By feeling the feelings, and then
moving on.

Keep Moving Forward

"Obstacles are a normal part of life and can help us grow our inner muscles." ~ Helene Lerner

Ask yourself:

Do I recoup from disappointments quickly?
Or do I stay depressed for days?

Act

Next time you aren't offered that job, for example, get support to move on and take action towards something better!

Self-Care

Take mini breaks throughout the day.
Work—recharge, work—recharge.
Get up and walk around. Don't keep
staring at your computer screen.
Self-care is not a part
of its programming.

Self-Care

"When you take time for yourself, you become more productive, not less." ~ Helene Lerner

Ask yourself:

Do I get headaches or feel neck or back pain during the day? Do I appreciate the value of taking time away from what I've been focusing on?

Act

When you think you can't take a break, do it anyway. You will be grateful you did.

Confront Your Fears

Deal with what you have been avoiding. If you don't, you're likely to stay stuck.

Confront Your Fears

"When fear rears its ugly head, look it in the eye, and give it a triple wink." ~ Helene Lerner

Ask yourself:

What am I afraid of right now?
Do I realize I have the strength to
move through any challenge?

Act

Do something that scares you today.

Let Go

When we tighten our grasp around
people, places, or things that are no
longer meant for us, we
hold ourselves back.

Let Go

*"When you hold on to the past, you do not have room
for new good to come into your life." ~ Helene Lerner*

Ask yourself:

*Do I give my power away by making someone or
something too important? Am I holding on to the way
I want things to be, rather than how they are?*

Act

When one door closes, they say, another will open.
Something better is coming!

Uncertainty

Change can feel disconcerting. We may resist it, but that won't help. Instead, if we remain open, we are usually led to bigger and better things.

Uncertainty

"You have the strength to move through the storms of life. Trust your inner compass." ~ Helene Lerner

Ask yourself:

Do I avoid discomfort?
Do I fill up my time with mindless activity?

Act

Stay with the discomfort of not knowing what's coming next. It won't kill you.

Think Bigger

Say "yes" to an opportunity coming your way. Think bigger about what you can achieve.

Think Bigger

"A strong woman realizes she is only using a fraction of her talents, and knows she is capable of much more. She is not afraid to step out of her comfort zone and lead in a new way." ~ Helene Lerner

Ask yourself:

Do I downplay what I can do?
Do I feel my greatness will impinge upon someone else?

Act

Take on this mantra:
"I deserve to do great things."

AFTERTHOUGHT

In my book[10] *In Her Power: Reclaiming Your Authentic Self,* I refer to the Fulfillment Manifesto, a list of what I consider to be our basic rights as women. Now, more than ever, its message continues to ring true: The person you're left with at the end of the day is you. Unfortunately, some of the places where we work, some of the people we may meet, may not share your desires for equity and growth. So in the end, it's up to you to reach deep within and never give up. To love yourself no matter what, express your talents, reach out for help when you need it, take care of your health, live abundantly, and create your life according to your own design.

It takes courage to live in a world changing so rapidly from one day to the next. But you are resilient, strong, and can lead the way when others retreat.

Thank you for being strong women who continue to push forward.

---

10. Lerner, Helene. *In Her Power: Reclaiming Your Authentic Self.* Atria Books, 2012.